delicious all day

Alex MacDonald

SAD PRESS

Bristol 2020

978-1-912802-37-1

for Sinead

Total and Complete Encounter

In my 24-hour trouser, I maintain a yacht demeanour
while a radio sings of pyjama mamas and melon papas.

This music made me grow at least three new leaves
and outside it's a great day to be a flag, to equivocally

mean something in fresh air, providing there isn't a moon.
What hopes do I hold while writing, while backing a car

over a cliff to park in another parallel? Each new poem
is a terrible posture on the same furniture. I ring you

on the seafront, foretelling of fresh hellos, waiting for a sign
like a pigeon flying in to a window. I found a direction

with my Geiger counter, there is so much there if you look.
The birds are repeating their catchphrases, with each

perfectly suiting this occasion. And however I peel this
orange, it remains delicious all day, delicious all night.

Indoor Voice

There's a public risk in living alone.
I'm convinced everyone has morals
like peeled potatoes in cold water.
I believe they are good.

I try to be light-hearted like a train toilet,
but I too am out of order. I hang around,
a haunted loofah of traditions. At night,
I scrub my monuments white, forever lucid.

Regrettably I'm full of the moods and I need
a lightness. The book I'm reading reminds me
of you, so maybe I will step out of my lighthouse
and eat my sandwiches on the rocks.

How would you like to be remembered?
I picture myself filled with green light,
each objection a seagull sitting on the sea,
hilarious and stoic. I say it is, and it's true.

Keep Apart Two Chevrons

a roadside majesty
two petrol stations
facing each other
one green and
one orange against
a purple sunrise
some are asleep
at slip roads
others are exhausted
in orthopaedic chairs
on their way
to molecular dramatics
with cat's eyes
hairpins and hard
shoulders to grip

Garden Remarks

Sweet signal in the leaves that something changed
between an image and a marble house,
where ghosts melt skin and finger pots, arranged.
Sorry to keep you waiting Minnie Mouse,
it is a young tradition I'm afraid
and what the painting said to me is this:
to levitate is love—a colonnade
between floating mystics, gentle abyss,
tadpole palace and gently-rooted weeds.
My head's a pond of koi anonymous
and I don't want to know what then proceeds.
I'll be naked among economists,
zombies will climb the fence, hot-tub ready.
On the menu: brain-flavoured daiquiri.

This Unnatural Valley While We Speak So Low

I'm not home right now – country roads go both ways

getting lost becomes contrary motion – a discipline of blurring out

hay bales five storeys high – a building of dead residents

a wall made now broken – I don't own anything here

me and two friends alone – our conversation stirs between us

I'm stunted by the possibilities – I hope it isn't obvious

walking is necessary and boring – what's there to think about

all this becomes sludge eventually – trees fall and birds melt

the future as moody teenager – everything black with flame detail

a spider watches me piss – eight eyes can't see shit

this open world those owls – unaware of the road's incline

we decide music beats poetry – bad poetry is about holidays

we throw these decisions out – what's important is your playfulness

how you interpret wild harps – wind through the telegraph wires

Your Body, Actually

for HC

There is only so much content at hand
and life has become very straightforward.

One option unfolds another: touch me and die.
Reassuring as a sinkhole, totally.

Seasons come on as a sausage restaurant,
hopeful, with all its blinding trinkets

and inherited imagery. No other replies needed.
We are living in a post-sacred age, so it's official,

nothing is sacred. It's official: leather pyjamas.
Go away, thoroughly, where winds have worn

deserts to a whistle, rocks shaped to a gesture.
How many rugs were pulled from under us?

And will we know a burning platform among
all this interference, this life of soft graft.

Hello Morning

I am heading North with shadows
travelling down a train carriage
and I'm tired of my feelings,
they are bound men in my basement:
there's no more to cut off.

I wanted to get in touch, a few
epiphany jams to stall an urge
out in the country. I'm trying
to be hopeful, open to affection.
That's enough about foam parties.

Blank Inside For Your Message

A featureless morning, a supermarket roof
of a day spent thinking in framed sunlight,

bare pages and what the windscreen knows.
Someone sings of entering your world like spring,

a new feeling in the get-go of radio noise,
and now I'm an iceberg breaking away

in bath water and wow these vacant prairies.
What came before this, moist handshake days

and coming home like an egg-heavy salmon?
Each noble idea segmented leaves a pith

and history only returns when fully extinguished,
a thought like a manager in their empty restaurant.

Tuesday's coming with a dirge knotted in its heart
but oh! these are the tiara wearing days my friends,

the long-sung note a tap whistles when filling a vase
showing the business end of flowers.

Brief Street

my coolest friend
this is the season
of small things

on brief street
aphids orbit
babies try vowels

and someone
is practicing
the clarinet

these evenings
are a dimmer
on full dim

my heart opens
its arms like
a mantis

what are you
making down
the corridor

a fish salad with
capers like a
newt's idea

a silent chorus
of pea shoots
under cellophane

On Seeing You With Our Friends on Instagram Stories

I'm at your table by accident, a chorus of haunted busts
in the museum where I night watch. A variety of laughs,
someone's trying out all the doorbells in a doorbell shop.
Lately I hardly meet your face. They're more your friends
and my friends now.

Garden City

isn't love like Letchworth
no hedges but topiary
fountains instead of streams
canopy corridors
leading to other ordered trees
the country's first roundabout
its thin options
to houses designed to be darling
tiny windows
awkward thatched rooves
every street a line-up of 70s footballers
these pink garage doors
closed and full of apparatus
a feeling I recognise
on a road called 'Paradise Is'
a plan that does not stay

Davachi Poems
i)   Mordents

other thoughts hold me up
if it isn't light on a brick wall
it's the shadow cast by a crane
a mark across the heart
or the surface of a pond
with its own green culture
what hinges do I swing on
which two rooms do I connect
the work floor and the nurse's office
a cellar with a fur coat of dust
and this flight of stairs
so frequently I am between two places
two ideas like the twin walls
of a trash compactor
helpfully reducing all options
to a single premise

ii)	Matins

there is a morning routine
little noises pitched low
garden birds hopping out of shadow
the sun saying something fresh
and small with its studied corona
I have been dreaming my watch
has teeth again and when
the wind hits the windows
it sounds like children singing
there is a deeper register today
I spill an egg and cats are breathing
this early hour has a fluttering
a movement among the ferns
I require a better knowledge
of what is being strained here
like water becoming coffee
an egg becoming an egg
I have learnt by heart
this dumb shuffling

Oh Baby, Telephone

We spent so long naming the cats
and now I realise it's talking to you
I miss most. All the wrong songs
now make sense, it's awful
for La Dolce Vita to mean anything
and worse to admit it here.
We talked while baking
on volcanic beaches
like emergency bacon,
walking parallel to canals
projecting starlight
and on our way to Plath's grave,
picking wildflowers for her.
A man jumped from behind her site
and spoke like he knew silence,
a bath running over perishing our ceiling.
Now, only Ryan Paris speaks to me
and even the sweet life is a snow globe
I chose to throw down the stairs.
I want to be alone or with you
hearing the cats' hallway monologues,
two tender weirdos
who think their names are 'hello'.
You are welcome always
in the lobby of my thoughts,
but I too am a grave man,
a gremlin at Christmas,
festive, tinkering with intent.
The days are longer, crueller than before
purple leaves finally puckering,

the original Hollywood of seasons
and this is my way of lighting
two cigarettes and offering one to you,
so don't let's ask for love
when all the best films
are conversations good enough
to watch on warm reels of tape
like a favourite story
told while walking.
I walk a lot these days,
listening to one voice
and before I join a darkness
I won't ask you about leaving or love
but I'm so alone in la dolce vita,
oh baby, telephone.

Let's Go Swimming

he thinks of water   how impossible it is
almost invisible   sucking up sound
   like someone being pulled out
of the atmosphere   someone who
sees all the blue in the earth at once

he thinks of how water is portrayed
in the movies   long marimba tones
skin-tight divers explore   fuzzy rocks
   fish look on in disbelief   he remembers
space station training montages   a block
of water the size of a house   filled
with spacemen   one is in the bathroom
another is having trouble at the front door

he looks at all the men wearing black shorts
   like censor strips blocking out indecencies
before the water shed   when the family
would be in the front room   eating hot dinners
   he thinks of the words   'water shed'
of aquatic lawn mowers   red eyes

he remembers the first pool   orange light
dim bulbs on a thick wooden ceiling
   only communal changing rooms   nothing
to distinguish one body   from the next
  dad's impatience at his discomfort

he thinks about breathing regularly   the day
ahead divided in to glassy hours   the people
he will have to say hello to

he remembers the old woman on the bus
    her trolley   bags falling out each side
how he thought about spaniel ears

    he pauses at the end of the pool
near a green drain   he thinks about
her tie-dye dress   her anguish at the bus
stopping   how she wanted to get home
how it was illegal for the bus to stop
so frequently   then each passenger's smile
unhooking   when she kept complaining
why was the bus stopping   where are they
    why wasn't she home yet   she created
her own force field of empty seats

in the slow lane   three pregnant women
    laughing   each of their bellies pointing
at the other   he thinks of the last scene
of Reservoir Dogs

he thinks of his mum   who is changing
into another woman   he remembers
her gear stick grip   how she drove out
into fields   into autumn mist to show
   how things were often obscured
a private land   unobtainable to us

he watches men swimming butterfly
and thinks of their houses of mirrors
    and certificates

he thinks about his body   how he isn't
who he wanted to be   he cannot make out
who that person is either

he moves through water for the last time
     it dries on his shoulders   leaving
a lemon smell   he thinks about the water
he leaves behind   its world and edges
     the unknown where it rolls off and out
through itself again   no one asked him
to imagine this free water

The Convenient Rip

people have their perforated edges
designed to tear apart
I am feeling the convenient rip
as the night offers its distractions
a cat discovers its reflection
a violet sky shrugs
and a gale breaks branches
that fall like fossilised lightning
some great power now diverted
how much can change overnight
a child may wake up to snow
or snails signing autographs
on a winter window
but underneath he is often
a boy with too many teeth
who knows how to be alone
you sit and talk to everything
personalities are endless
each chair every carpet
has their thick moods
and understated yearnings
stains like birth marks
becoming a pattern of life
I try to begin at the beginning
a copy made of water
allow me to take this shape
be reflective and slow to change
offer an image back to you
that breaks and remains still

Notes and Acknowledgements

A number of these poems take their titles and lines from elsewhere, including songs and writings by Arthur Russell, Asha Bhosle, Marilyn Manson, Charles Dickens, Ryan Paris, Lightning Bolt, Laurie Anderson and The Plastics.

The *Davachi Poems* are named after and inspired by songs by Sarah Davachi

Thank you to the editors of *Prototype II*, *Hotel*, *For Every Year* and *PERVERSE* and *Bath Magg* who published versions of these poems.

Thank you also to Rebecca Tamas, for looking at an early draft of these poems, Helen Charman for her encouragement and editorial support and Will Harris for his guidance and introducing new work for me to consider. Most of all, thank you to Sinead Evans for her support, care and inspiration throughout the writing of these poems.

Lightning Source UK Ltd.
Milton Keynes UK
UKHW020108250221
379270UK00005B/250

9 781912 802371